"I like an Indian better dead than living. I have never in my life seen a good Indian - and I have seen thousands - except when I have seen a dead Indian."

James M. Cavanaugh, May 28, 1868,
House of Representatives, Washington, D.C

Dedicated to
my grandparents and great grandparents-
Lorne & Dorothy, Giles & Ruth
Nettie, Belva & Byrd

PRAYERS AND INVOCATIONS

CEREMONIES FOR THE DEAD 1

the time has come
to let the dead come in.

they have waited long enough
for you to remember their names.

these sunken arms once held you up
so don't pretend they are strange guests,
unsought visitations in the night.

it is you who has called them here
and you are the only one
who can give them peace.

see their bloated tongues move,
each has a story to tell,
bruised lips rustling together as the night
gathers them home with damp fingers.

look at the familiar faces
but ignore the missing limbs and decaying flesh;
they are beautiful in their disintegration

your ancestors have come to visit
and they are hungry so you must feast
the murmuring bones.

offer them yourself,
no lover has ever touched you deeper
than they will, as they remember their words
through your descendant body.

come on child,
the dead have come for you
and they will not be denied
their last chance to speak.

CEREMONIES FOR THE DEAD 2

if you want to conduct
an Indian ceremony for the dead,
gather a long white sheet
and one coil of rope.

cut down a few branches from the nearest cedar,
strip the needles from the wood,
and crush them between your fingers.

breathe in the scent of the resulting paste,
as you slide warm hands over the chilled body
paying special attention to the lifeless hands,
heavy limbs, and pallid lips.

light a waterproof match from your jeans
and toss the weak flame into ashtray,
smoulder it with dried sage, a few strands of your hair,
and put it out with a dash of whiskey.

gather the sheet and toss it over the body,
tie it on tightly so everything is covered,
no loose fingers or exposed toes, just one blank
bundle of nothing.

find the tallest tree in the back yard
and using the coil of rope, make a noose
for the feet.

Truss up the woolen sack
like an oversized cocoon, strain your back
until the tree branch is bowed from the weight
but remember to tie off the rope securely.

once properly hoisted, the corpse should rot
in the wind and rain for at least a couple months,
maybe years depending on your seasonal climate,
and you should make no attempt to release it
to the cold ground.

do not mention the deceased's name
for a least 13 moons,
give away everything left
including houses, clothing, memories
and children.

every couple of days,
walk out to your backyard and light up a smoke,
as you stand underneath the tallest tree
and watch your loved one disintegrate into vital fluids,
lumps of bone shrinking as the once white sheet
turns red, blue, then black.

feel nothing, except regret
and a slow appreciation for the gestational cycle
of death.

CEREMONIES FOR THE DEAD 3

in the church of my mother's people,
a thin slatted wooden building high in the Appalachian mountains
with no discernible colour save for the wind bleached grey
covering the jagged land,

they keep death sacred
by singing hymns in low voice
as the mourners wail their grief
from prostrate benches at the front row.

here death is tired, a familiar friend
and the funeral service is more ritual than remembrance,
an inherited ache which keeps seasons and time
better than any miner's calendar.

menfolk have their own side in the chapel,
a row of wooden pews and blackened faces,
years of hunting in the underworld keeps spines bent
but the faces are upright, proud in the watery light
as another generation falls over dead
before them.

the women nod their heads
when the backwoods minister speaks.
the children are hushed by a sea of spinster aunts
and wiry older sisters, everything kept in check
by female hands, guiding the invisible currents
of life toward some unseen place.

after the service, the body is placed in a wooden box,
roughly nailed shut at the corners but otherwise
indistinguishable from any other company crate,
and the entire community climbs a high hill
to bury what remains.

every year since,
the soil creeps further down the mountain side
and reclaims the grave markers, successive generations
wandering the graveyard will find no trace
of their ancestors left in this earthy crag
only small bright blue flowers which bloom
for a couple months in the spring.

CEREMONIES FOR THE DEAD 4

If you kill a halfbreed,
make sure to dispose of the evidence
in a culturally appropriate manner.

I recommend reciting high latin mass
while some old Indian bag lady dances
counter clockwise in jeans and beat up fringe jacket.

give a brief eulogy in Ojibway or Cree
but change every fourth noun to French
and smile broadly to the attending ghosts
because every dead Indian loves
a consummate salesman.

make sure you pay attention to the deceased's mixed heritage
by telling a couple off hand jokes about how Indian women
are good in the bush but hairless in the sack.

be careful not to overstate how much Indian blood
ran through their veins or you'll make them sound barbaric.
just dress the simple details by changing trapper into freelance guide
or say they lived in a shack because it brought them
closer to God's creation.

don't forget to go back into the census records
with an quill pen dipped in black ink
so you can scratch out previous generations
and leave confusing annotations like CNRW in the margins.

be sure to correct the clerk's handwriting
by checking off the columns for mulatto or white
if their coloring was passable.

if you killed them in a remote location
I suggest digging a shallow grave with a rifle butt
so the wild animals can have something to eat
when the freeze sets in.

the worst you could do would be to give them a proper burial
because of the bureaucratic headache you'll encounter.
no good Christian graveyard accepts Indian corpses
and you can't take them back to their ancestral reserves
where memory falls apart after one generation gone.

ignore any feelings of guilt or empathy
which may disrupt your normally cheerful disposition
as there are literally thousands of halfbreeds still left
and the government encourages killing at least one
per hunting season.

GRAVE DIGGING

Let's go grave digging,
you and me.

we can go tonight,
under the last moon of summer
when the ground is damp, soil loose
from the weight of rainfall and humidity.

we'll take your pickup truck,
toss a couple spades in the back
and slide up the deserted highway
like a couple of thieving Injuns
on horseback.

find one of those Indian burial grounds,
hidden under rows of corn in a farmer's field,
and start exhuming the bodies randomly
while the wind whistles past our jeans.

you can catalogue the individual bones,
femur, pelvis, and skull ridge in one pile,
arrow heads and cracked pottery in another
as I thrust my fingers through the dirt
to pull up handfuls of our ancestors.

I made some sandwiches and dug out
a bottle of cheap wine strong enough
to get us good and drunk while we work
so the dead will see we know the proper rituals
to honour the decaying underworld.

afterwards, sweaty and covered in dust,
like two cowboys riding on the great plains,
we can hold hands or just fuck beside the exposed corpses
'cause even the dead need a good show
once every hundred years or so

if you really love me,
you'll time your orgasm perfectly
just as the moon rises up from behind
dark clouds and sweeps the graves
with that silver light which makes
the bones dance once again

doesn't that sound like a fun time,
baby, you and me lying under the stars
surrounded by lakes and lakes of skeletons
finally brought home in the lodges
of our euphoric bodies.

MOOSHKAHAN / THE FLOOD

"Mii piinihs ahpane ahkiini
oki waapantaan ayanimiyahkiiwaninik."
-Williams Jones, *Cree Legends and Narratives*

Until he saw the earth of his seed
extended away indefinitely,
there was nothing
but corpses in cold water,
a slow turning darkness living
in the deep.

he said a long time ago
the earth was a fragment of dirt,
clay and silica shifting beyond
the point of creation, idle speculation
gathering on the underside
of his shoes.

us humans, sleeping limbs splayed out
over beds of sweetgrass, stars moving
through our ghostly bodies,
waiting for him to return
from the sheath of night time.

not only his hands touched us,
his tongue against our damp skin
and fingers slipping inside
our bodies like minnows darting
from shadow to shadow
away from the sun

his cock made flesh with urgency,
seeking our centers, drawing in air and moisture
in stillborn lungs, the corridors of blood

igniting in a slow burn as he kissed
our misshapen lips.

his seed dark and gentle, pressed into
our ribs as the outline of bones,
cartilage taking form
from his careful ministrations.

each separate act of penetration
creating one distinct galaxy
in the body of a soul.

LAND OF THE DEAD

I imagine the dead congregate
behind the edges of the present moment
like scorned children being punished
for some unknown crime, eyes full of remorse
and begging to let back in.

they have no homes but the ones
we give them, stone and metal corridors
where unmoving and bound, they rot
into nothing.

we've driven them from the day
with our casual indifference to the spectral fingers
clutching at our sleeves, like forgetful parents
whose ghostly children wander off into oncoming traffic
and disappear forever.

Even the night is no longer theirs alone,
the incandescent brilliance of our corner stores
and 24 hour diners cloaking us from their eyes,
turning them inward and sullen.

but where is the land of the dead,
the place they gather and tell their stories
in low voices, calling the dusk down
from the birch bark lodges of their mothers?

if you want to know where to look
for them, hoping to catch them by surprise
as they boil river water for their morning tea,
lift up one hand and trace the outline
of your spine.

follow the contours of hands and feet
as you step, memory by memory,
into the land of your body
where the dead lie waiting.

BEAVER PONDS

not a natural feature
of the land, a beaver pond is a cesspool.

a hundred years of silt sunken
with the corpses of poplar
and cedar limbs, a cemetery for trees
where unseen, the forces of earthly decay
gather.

a shallow circle of pine
skirts the water's grasping touch,
a thin boundary between the living
and the dead as the banks shift,
soil receding as the water swells with season,
the tireless fall of rain.

under the surface of thick brown water,
everything is broken down, rotted out to its essential gasses.
if you put a hand down, leaning over the edge and sliding
your arm into the damp, you could press against the bottom
and feel sulphur, the tongues of leeches, and wood crumble
beneath your touch.

if you step into a beaver bond,
by the tributaries or in the wallowing bones of the swamp,
you could sink past the last century of environmental change,
disappear into the muck of time itself.

our human way is to seal
bodies in the cold earth, maintain separate
distinctions between the dead, saying this was
one person and here lies another.

beaver ponds are nature's way of denying any private sorrow -
everything comes to the same darkness,
trees, soil, fish, and insect.

even the makers,
gods of their dissolving kingdom, will die
and fold into the depths. beaver tails silent,
unmoving as flesh warps, eaten by
the press of water, sliver worms, and the watchful eye
of the moon.

CEMETERY

the resonant pause
of earth drawing moisture
down from the flat sky,
pools of stale air
creating eddies of warmth, coolness
a brief movement between bodies, nothing more
and nothing less.

Mourners' heads like trampled grasses,
tilt forward, bend at the middle, fall back
as if a spine was another excuse
for undignified behavior.

a sea of white starched shirts
shimmers in and out of vision, a mirage
of cotton water tempting the dryness in my mouth.
I watch brown stains gather at the hems, evaporate in
minutes as even sweat refuses to linger here.

my father is praying, his heavy voice
as weary as the trees, drought leaving everything
brittle a long wooden coffin,
raised by cords over a shallow hole in the ground, is waiting
for an end to the heat.

when they finally lower it
and shovel clops of damp sod back
home, I imagine I can hear the grateful
corpse sigh. as my mother grabs my hand,
drags me into the musky leather interior
of our car, I cast one final look
at the sleepy cemetery.

a part of me wonders
if the humidity is a human
emotion the dead no longer feel

once safely across the river dividing
our lives from theirs.

do they long to taste
the salt from their pores, feel the stagnant
weight of a hundred summers
once more?

NINOONTAN /I HEAR IT

the voices you hear
are not the tongues of wind,
whispering between the birches
and calling your name.

not the rustle of the night's lips
against your skin, the cool trace
of restless stars as they shift across
the boundaries of bone you call
a skeleton.

not the slow current of breath
sliding down your wet throat
to rise and fall in the embrace
of muscle and memory.

not the sounds of animals
the low calls sitting on the edge
of what you can comprehend
or give name and shape to.

not the sky suspended
from the horizon like cedar boughs
hung to dry in the high reaches
of the past.

not even your hands turning
over the weight of damp logs
can speak the language of decay
better than the ones who are loose tonight.

they have come down to lie
in the roof of your mouth, swollen
and heavy with moisture as you try
to spit them back into the lake water.

if you swallow and close your teeth
against their bitter taste, the voices
will consume you like a split fish
bleeding out on a riverbank rock.

listen to the sound
spread its wings in the blackness
and beat like bone beads
moving in one great rattle.

can you hear it?
the dead standing up in their shadowy lodges
as what was forgotten begins to sing
in the emptiness of the night.

NAME (STURGEON)

Brother,
I want to call you kin,
spit in your salty mouth and bind you
to my flesh.

I hear the rush of the lake,
feel the water rising against my thighs, calling me to you.

 Five thousand years you have swum
beneath my ancestors' feet, our birch
canoes clouds in your murky sky.

Others call you sinful in the dark waters,
shadow on the river before our human hands descended,
churned the damp to bring you blinking into
light and air.

Teach me to carve my ribs
into the shape of you, the thin needles
which compress, contort their way through your spine.
Only my lungs hold me back now,
the wet sacks of membrane and
mucus lacking your folding center,
the way you can collapse yourself
with the river's pressure.

Skin can easily become scale,
muscles reworked to be narrow bands
of current, purpose changed to carry me
through the winding corridors of water and reed.

My heart has never been dry,
and blood is just another liquid of salt and memory.
A river is a mind, a lake, a brain of sunlight and
stony bottom, pieces of life I already
know.

Brother, if you take underneath
time, past the point of memory
where all sight is blind
and feeling cold, numb by
the weight of a million seasons
of rain,

I will become yours until I die,
feast your bones in winter
and spread my hands among
the halls of your ancestors.,

singing your name with
my human tongue, calling
all the songs of your family together again
in the dark.

PIITAAPAN / THE DAWN

you say the dawn rests on the hinge of time,
the moment of light lifting from deep blue
to silver is no trick of horizons, but of centuries rolling
back like the waters of Lake Superior.

the blackness lingering on the earth
is the coal mines of my mother's father,
a doorway to the dynamited tunnel of mountain walls
and thin iron rail tracks, where the air is clouded
with a darkness more real than any other absence of light.

the deep blue, where the darkness has surrendered
to the pressure of waking birds and call of wild things,
is my gookum's ghost, giving up ground in death as in life
to the burrowing hunger her children feel for their father's
fiery gaze.

let the yellow sky be the burnished brass of ocean steamers,
carrying my grandfather's ancestors to Halifax
but leave me the silver ribbon of light,
keep it away from the clutching hands of the dead
and out of memory's pocket.

the human in me wants to hold on
to whatever small part of time
is mine alone.

GOOD INDIAN

take off your skin,
flay the muscle
from the heart.

scrape the tendon
until you can thread
a bone needle.

sew yourself
to a corpse,
stitch the dead.

fall asleep in a swamp
so the weight of death
can pull you under.

you will remember
what it means to be
a good indian.

FEASTING THE MURMURING BONES

INTO THE LAND OF THE DEAD

take me with you
behind the falling down barn,
the one with the sheet metal roof lifting
up in the morning wind.

let's bring baloney slices in our pockets
a couple of handfuls of yellow seed
and leftover chunks of bacon grease
to litter along our way.

these little pieces of us
can be left behind and forgotten
without feeling any sense of loss,
we've both had enough of grief
to last us a couple of long winters.

you can show me where the stream begins
and the river ends, the boundaries of land
which shape your world are important
to remember - keep them fixed
in your wandering mind.

we have no need for words
this last time. I can read your body
as well as any horizon, the shifting light you wear
is enough for me to follow you through
the trap lines of memory.

gookum, I said I would return
to those far away summers of childhood
but you left before I could come back
and they closed up your house and sold
everything.

this is what we have left,
the land of the dead breathing around us
and one last moment in the morning air
to remember each other.

RODEOS

he died flicking channels,
hunting through the late night informercial haze
for one good rodeo.

alone in his stiff backed leather chair,
chewing tobacco stained , losing ground
under a sea of cigarette ashes, he snuffed out
one click away from the rumble
of over fed hooves.

no one witnessed his inelegant fall,
the dog twenty years dead, whiskey bottle gone dry
and all the lights turned off.

when my goookum found him,
arms tucked in around his chest and the tv still flickering on static,
she poured herself a drink and sat in the kitchen until the sun tumbled
out of the Michigan sky.

the aunties thought it was simple shock,
her brain struggling to make sense of the last cowboy
to die in recent memory

but I always figured her and the bulls
had a moment of silent communication, the low lulling in the red steel barnyards
sliding through the television window into her small house,
each damaged party holding vigil over the remains of a bitter contest
where outlasting means more than any pitiful claim
to ten second glory.

every rodeo rider knows,
sooner or later, you take one big dive
when no one's watching except
for the bulls

those long suffering beasts of burden,
waiting for their one chance
to spit on your grave.

BORDERS

morning came in grey light,
rain following us across the border
that sat between my father's pain
and his forgetting

my gookum standing in the dirt yard,
growing small in the rearview mirror,
her youngest son trying not to look back
as we sped down the gravel road.

every summer for ten years, he came back
for a week of penance, fixing light bulbs
and buying groceries as my grandfather watched
over his disrupted kingdom from a beatup lazy boy

gookum made us weed the garden,
trying to keep us kids outside
away from what lumbered about inside
and slipping me dollar bills whenever I found
one of his buried whiskey bottles

the last morning, we left early
'cause grandpa came back from town
drunk with his leather belt wrapped
around gnarled fists and we hid upstairs
while my father had his last childhood battle.

the aunties were called in,
suitcases packed and hurried goodbyes given,
and I watched my gookum grow dim,
hooded eyes turning quiet and deep
as we shuffled away for another long year

we heard after we drove away
that he kept her on her feet
until the veins broke, made her boil
a couple of hot dogs while the blood gathered
in arthritic ankles.

they admitted her to hospital in Indian River
but sooner or later, she had to go back home
and he was waiting with the familiar offerings
of his hands, ghostly bruises blooming
over her face like summer ragweed

my father, hearing the second hand news,
kept his peace and didn't call
for months.

the distance between him and her so vast
not even driving for eight hours straight
could cross it.

INDIANS

I come from a long line
of Indians with too much anger
to beg for forgiveness for things left unsaid,
whiskey bottles left out when visitors came
in from town.

my grandmother's an Indian
and my grandfather too, they both
bit the hand that feeds 'em
and spit the pieces back.

seventy lean years
of poverty, refusing the government's monetary
admission of guilt, they're still too proud
to call themselves anything
but free.

one time, driving past the rez,
my gookum told me she'd rather
be dead than be an Indian.

watching them sitting there, rocking to death
with cigarettes lit and television
on, not speaking to each other
as much as speaking through,
I wanted to say,

"well, you got your wish,
 didn't you?"

in the distance,
a car slows down on the road, flicks its
lights on and off.

silently, I tell it

"just keep on driving by,

you won't find any trace
of nobility in this
dark place."

THE BITTERS WAYS

I blame you for nothing,
not even your heavy silence which filled up rooms
and lingered long after your death.

the violence you made your life around
was more than your husband's fists
but started in your mother's womb,
dark and bloody from the beginning.

the original hurt blossomed deeper
than bruises on your children's skin,
seeped into their bones like cloudy ink
and coated the membranes of their eyes,
blinding all your descendants equally.

did you think yourself brave,
to stand against my grandfather's anger
while the children ran out of the house
and through the bush to hide in the forest's shadows?

or did you believe an Indian woman's place
was to be a clay wall that generations of men
could try to climb, shatter with their hands
when age and winter's freeze set in?

you had to know the truth,
that your children would fear him
but hate you more for the bitter ways
you failed to protect them.

could you see the line of us,
your descendants stretching out across the night sky,
like a toppled fence of barbed wire stars?

you must have seen in dreams
the sight of our faces, bruised by different hands

but struck by the same worn out shame of being the losers
in this black and white world of cowboys and Indians?

or was your vision consumed by your mother's people,
marching through Minnesota with rifles at their backs
as they began to forget themselves?

Gookum,
I blame you for nothing
but the questions you left behind.

FRAGMENTS

burn the trees
and break the ground open,
slide your fingers between the horizon
and the land. taste
the lake water, spit it
over your shoulder.

gather the stars, the sun
a dim flame in your
ribcage, even the moon
can be captured, sunk
in your mouth like a fish head
swallowed whole.

ink out the curve
of hills, valleys surrendering
to your roaming tongue,
renaming every piece
of my land, myself.

take the children, saplings
to bend against borders
of nations, countries of birches
splitting at the root, weave them
in your image, their bodies
a lodge of nothing.

press your fingers
into my grandmother's brain,
squeeze out the blood
from every memory, slap
the imprint of your palm
against cheek bone, leave
a mark by which to know
your hands.

even my father's spine,
mother's womb can be your
bridges, storehouse of rotting
timbers to lay the train tracks,
carry you over the mountains
to undiscovered ocean,
waiting for you to
finally arrive.

one by one, you can have
everything in sight, even the imagined
and the real are grasses under your
boot step, as there is nothing your god does not give you

he asks only for the fragments
you leave behind.

FIGHTING WORDS

they call us
pretty little dirty words
you could drive a bullet
through.

but don't you dare call my grandfather
anything but a bastard. his mother may be a half-breed
fur bride but goddamn it, he's a pure blood
fucker too stubborn to die and too drunk to care.
kicked out of kindergarden for sharing moonshine from
a metal thermos, he hasn't sobered up
yet.

watch your mouth around my gookum,
she's got a mean glare and arthritis
in her hip. I remember her brown hands
pressed tight to mine, drawing me
past the watchful eyes of strangers in
the grocery store, forty long years of living
in this redneck town and she's still
not one of 'em

you're wasting time on my father,
his stubborn denial of anything savage thicker
than lake ice, shouting at me
when I was a child, fists swinging
at the absences his father left
him and the only thing he can
reach is my face

I'm your best bet
for any expletives you've saved up
the long winter. these blue eyes and
pale skin hide a forked tongue, heathen mind
lying in wait

for your mouth to open,
watch you drink your own poison
down.

DROUGHT

I was born in the heat of summer,
the hottest on county records,
as if the sun knew my destiny
would be fire and the leaving of ashes.

all over the county,
wells went dry. wild fires
spread in back lots, asphalt split
open and ran free of the roads.

the fields, slack jawed and pawing
at ground, went unwatered for months. No
clouds came even though the farmers spit
in their hands, held the soil between their palms.

corn stalks tumbled under
the ploughing step of cows and no one bothered
to call them back in.

everyone was plain old beat. You could walk from one
end of the town to the other side without
seeing a soul, clouds of dust providing
the only voices.

born early, the sun rising, climbing
up the barn beams to stretch out against
the thirsty sky, I cried for months
and was always restless.

the only baby born to the town
sunken by the weight of drought,
how could I be anything

but the eye of the land, hollow
brown circle of earth, staring back at the light
and praying for the rain to
darken me?

DOUBT

I have to say
what has not been said.

how many years of sin
hides behind our eyes, peers out
of photographs and clings to our bodies
like a shroud of black silk,
masking the shape
of our doubt.

did he take them one by one
into the bedroom, down the long hallway
I remember from childhood, the one
with holes in the panelling and mouse traps
buried along the corridor?

was he gentle or rough
when whiskey loosed his hands
from their daily prayers, let his fingers cross
the boundaries of kin and desire to find
some new and exciting land
in their descendant flesh

did he gaze across the dining room table,
proud adventurer at the edge of a great expanse,
another country to discover in his children's bodies,
fertile soil to break ground, sow the seeds of sorrow
deeper than any metal plow could furrow.

did my gookum linger over the supper dishes,
washing each one twice until gleaming, the porcelain bones were laid to rest
in the oak cabinets he carved so long ago,
before he found more precious woods to shape,
cut along the seams and bind together
in the dark.

the details may not matter in the end,
no need for precision when the heavy blows of violence
have battered the faces beyond human comprehension
into the land of doubt, where truth is a privilege
of full bloods and whites.

it is enough for me
to say we are half breeds
and what was done to us
by these long centuries of loss

is no worse than what we have done
to ourselves.

ROADS

how long have we wandered these roads
only to find they end with ourselves?

If you took me on a long walk
past the mounds and over the gravel hill,
could we find what remains of us
lying scattered in the ditches
and hanging on fence posts?

our stories have left us tonight,
gone off to find the ears of strangers
ready to listen, more determined to give
meaning where we have seen nothing.

we live such small lives, taking nourishment
from our isolation and calling it wise to befriend absence
while the willow trees' branches creep closer to the ground
as stars move past us and the night forgets our names.

we have not been brave,
standing at the shore as the waters carry
the bodies out to the islands, taking our regret
past our immediate reach but leaving it close enough
to look towards in the fading light.

we have hidden the graves and burned the leftovers,
spread the ashes over our faces to confuse the angry ghosts
but still they come hunting, sniffing at our doorsteps
as we lie in bed, jealously guarding the remnants
of themselves from our slow digesting.

gookum, you and I have gone out to smoke
in the heavy night air, lighting up and taking deep drags
as we walk along the dirt road running by your house
but our packs are empty and it is time to face the attending spirits
we cannot banish.

both you and I know
the only way these roads run is back.

ACCOUNTING

open the doors
and bring the serpents inside
to curl around our feet, burrow into our lungs
and bite the stories loose.

poison is the fiery promise
burning in our eyes tonight,
we have come together
to sing the bones awake.

dead indians have no shame
and our halfbreed tongues are clipped
short and deadly so we can finally speak
without fear.

boil the cedar needles
and pour out all the whiskey
across the floor so we can drink
the smell of it.

the basswood is dry enough to carve
and we brought out the good knives
to dig into its fleshy pulp, scrape out
a hollow for the voices to gather.

stretch the hide across the basswood circle
as we pound the kitchen table,
remember the songs given to us
during the long winter sleeping in the snow.

the menfolk can sing first
while my gookum sits by the window
and cleans her rifle for when the government
decides to drop by.
everyone is here, casting long shadows
in the stove fire light as the night winds
circle our house, sneak through cracks
and whistle in the cracked bones.

we dug up the skeletons this afternoon,
spent all week cooking and tonight,
for the first time in a hundred years,
we are going to sing each other whole.

THE FAMILIAR FACES

Indian lips and halfbreed cheeks,
we turn to catch the moment's eye.

firelight diffused across our skin
hides the imperfections, the lighter sons
and the darker daughters become the same colour
in the late summer evening, like polished cedar wood
appearing from behind the carver's hands

we are dressed in our traditional regalia,
blue jeans and pressed cotton shirts stained to a damp yellow
by tobacco spit and cigarette ash,
as my grandfather glares down the uneasy photographer
with the look of an old warrior too drunk to give a fuck

hands crossed, faces upturned
the daughters are steady in their resolve,
determined to have one good photograph to chuck
against the wall when anger overwhelms sentiment

even the sons are trying hard to keep still,
legs stiff and backs braced against each other
like tired bulls in a stockade, each one betting
on who crumbles first and is swallowed by the whole

the only familiar face with nothing to hide
is my gookum as she sits, calm and certain
of her family's continued unraveling, the trauma
spinning faster out of our hands the tighter we grasp
on to it.

she shares a private humour
with the attending ghosts, the ones
the camera only partially captures in dark blots,
white specks on the filament of our bodies.

the joke is still funny if you can understand the irony
of half-breeds dressed up and wasting a perfectly good sunday
to capture the photographic evidence of what our ancestors
did and did not do, what they said and couldn't say.

BOTTOM

I am a bottom
diver.

an underwater dreamer
whose lungs expand with the song
of memory, taken down past
the surface tensions.

give the birds their lonely skies,
wings blackened by evening
and fluttering against the stars,
oversized moths transfixed in the deathly glimmer
of what cannot be reached by flesh alone.

leave the churning land,
the curves of hills which carry bones
up to greet the rising sun as trees,
forests of skeletons growing florescent green
as their spines burrow into the soil
to gather up life.

the cities, burial mounds and temples can be forgotten
in the underwater world, there is no need for any gods
but the ones of decay, oxygen transmuted from the breath of fire
into a cloak of liquid, the container in which everything is consumed
slowly by the gentle hands of bacteria.

here, I am home
in the dark and weight of the past
and no other being can see so clearly the expanse
of lake floor spreading out around me.

I am the only one left
who reaches the bottom without drowning,
the others suffocate on the absence of air like stillborn children
as the waters reject their careless incursions
with a deadly patience.

but I reach past the silt,
the blue darkness of the lake
to touch the bottom, the point where memory rests
waiting for one last moment in the gleaming light.

DARKNESS

the dark is more alive
for the dead who inhabit it.

the earth casting down a shroud,
darkness swelling up from behind the sky
to reach out damp hands and pull the curtains
of forgetting down over the slumped houses,
the deserted street corners casting long shadows
and humming with the silence of ghosts

the secret dark, mystery of what shuffles about
when all human eyes turn away from windows
and clutch tightly to their flickers of warmth,
our stolen fire as the sun abandons us
to glisten in the lives of other, more interesting, people

still the dark is not made lonely by human absence,
does not falter and question meaning like a child cast off
without the guiding arms of parents, the roots of familial ties
severed by the coming dusk, the dark is no orphan
from the light

instead, the dark goes larger, reaches out
through the windows and locked doors to claim
another form of radiance in the human minds
which turned away from it in the evolutionary leap
from midnite survivour to hallowed conquerer of the day

if memory has a home, it is here in the dark,
the invisible wiring of the brain cloaked by bone
and flesh as what is precious gathers, collects
on the underside of the eyes's light.

GODS OF MY FATHERS

"I will lift up my eyes to the hills/
from whence comes my help?"

-*Psalm* 121:1,

LOOK TO THE HILLS

Oh lord of my father,
keeper of tattered red hymn books
and the sun falling on a
polished wooden floor, do you
see me?

I am waiting
in the deepening dark
of this old church, brick and prayer
raised up against rows of corn, the bleating
of sheep in the pasture singing
your reluctant praises

above me, the rows of pews are
huddling together like old farm women waiting for
the next visitor, a brief moment of warmth,
purpose rediscovered.

I can hear the shuffling footsteps
of my mother's gait, her small frame somewhere
beneath me in the concrete basement, a broom
in constant vigilance against the gravel dust
of the small town she is buried in.

I sing to you, oh god
of the meek, of my father sitting
in his office, piecing together passages
of a kind of truth, blind to the other reality
awakening in my tender spine, my shaking
hands a lesson in weakness, vulnerability
no angels can conquer.

Can I climb up the tilting altar, raise
my hands one stained window ledge
to another, lift my heavy body to the height
of your love, the circle of glass by the oak trees,

a window to your heavenly sky
and wave, my maker?

If I look to the hills, those
dusty red wheat fields shaped by
your children's labors, their sweat an offering
to your mysterious cycles of rain, drought, and
inflation, will you come to me?

In thunder and lighting, in storm
and fury, god of the earthly salt,
will you appear in robes of white,
reach out your hand and press the bruise
on my shoulder, the mark your deacon left behind
when he held me against the cold
tiled floor, will you?

oh christ of my family,
who brings the rains and raises the waters,
can you drown my shame, the knowledge of man
in his hunger, lust for what is closest to you?

I am no child
anymore. And you, oh god
of men, are no god either. Let the
trumpets proclaim your death,
father of nothing.

the night is here, my mother is
calling my name as I lift myself off
the floor, up into the electric light
and away from you.

I waited at your doorstep, all day
after he left me alone downstairs, bitter caramel
candy in my mouth,

and god,
I can't wait any longer.

ADVICE FOR ABUSED CHILDREN

the most important thing to remember
is everything was your fault.

don't trust the friendly social worker
whose office is littered with framed photographs
of her happy family.

she only works here to remind you
that there are other children who can hear
a door latch lifting in the deep night
without grabbing the kitchen knife
hidden under the pillow and praying
to a deaf god who likes to watch.

try to forget about the childhood friends
who invite you to sleepovers and stay up late
watching horror movies while their parents benevolently
make microwave bags of popcorn and tell you
to come over more often.

they can never be anything but a slap in the face
and you get enough of that at home.

investigate all possible routes out of the house
and make sure you never lock any of the bedroom windows
because the rooftop is the safest place in the event
of an unexpected violation.

pick a favorite place in the surrounding neighborhood
so you have somewhere to wander around after school
before you go home to the next beating.

if you have any sudden desires to escape
by breaking down and telling school officials,
you should remind yourself that you are liar
who deserves every rough word
and sharp jab.

they will only call your parents
and politely ask them if they have ever hit you
more than once on any area other than
the ass.

your best bet is to find an overly sympathetic friend
whose parents work as doctors or teachers
so you can hide out at their house for a couple of days
until the charm of helping the less fortunate wears off
and the reality of just how fucked up you really are
becomes clear.

whatever you do,
never forget to stop fighting
and just let it happen as many times
as it needs to.

an active resistance will only make the shame
of losing worse.

honestly speaking,
the best advice I can give you
is to drown yourself at birth.

ADVICE FOR ABUSED CHILDREN 2

the waters will accept your offering
of flesh and shame.

paper thin lungs collapsing
as you start to drown, skin
turning blue and translucent
like stars rising at dusk

the world will take a step away
and give you time to mourn
what you have not been given
by the living and dead

the cool hands of death,
sliding between your armpits
to lift you up to the water's surface,
will cover the bruises and scars

the price of your survival dissolving
as the land begins to forget your step,
the pressure of your life gone from the rocky trails
and missing from the trees

you will discover an afterlife
floating in the shallows, face down
to watch the movement of shimmering fish
and thin algae as they reclaim your corpse

those years of hiding are gone
in the brilliance of lake water,
the combination of dark and damp
soaking the hurt out of your bones

the footsteps you heard
outside your bedroom door
are silent now, even the blows
you couldn't dodge have fallen limp
as you dance from sorrow into joy

at home in the deepening waters
where even pain can't breathe
and memory drowns under the steady lap

of current, pressure, and release.

ADVICE FOR ABUSED CHILDREN 3

death has many faces
and one of them is ours.

see our eyes follow strangers
like hungry dogs limping home
to cradle bones beneath their teeth,
afraid of theft from even the most gentle visitors.

our hands are restless, we catch and twist
the moment between our fingers like smokers
who roll their own tobacco into thin needles
hoping it will burn away slow and steady

everything is measured, kept for bad times
and stockpiled against the invisible menace
which radiates in our bodies, beats inside our ribs
like a shadowy moth against a lampshade

we lose friends and lovers with the same hurt
as losing strangers, spare change, and coupons
but we predict the coming absence with the accuracy
of an archer, striking the exact moment they leave
from months and miles away

we feel no hope except when some idiot,
hooked on their normalcy like a cheap high,
gives us a reason to long, a small desire
which calls out like a crow, drawing a chorus
of black sounds from the watching trees

they want us to lie,
wear the masks of promise
to cover the deficient gaze,
the absence we feel
in everything.

but we must remind them,
softly as to small children,
death has many faces
and one of them is ours.

ADVICE FOR ABUSED CHILDREN 4

there are some gifts
children never ask for
and don't deserve.

a christmas which never ends,
each present discovered in secret
in church basements, under blankets
and over mattresses.

we are the ones who will be unwrapped,
our jeans unbuckled and shirts pulled off
as the swollen hands search to loose
the bows of our bodily pleasure

they are disappointed
in how fast our bodies bloom,
the value of our gifts diminishing
with each passing year.

but no one stops to ask
why we cry at birthday parties
when the real presents appear,
bright and shining in the red foil paper
and filled with promise.

somehow we know, young but certain,
that the gifts other children receive
are exactly what we wanted but someone,
somewhere, fucked up and left us

this useless shame instead.

SUNDAY SERVICE

my father's voice is divining
his congregation. here and there
he senses the devil's business.

more poet than minister,
he weaves baritone prayers, lamentations of the flesh
delivered by note, intonation alone
enough to redden guilty faces.

everyone turns away but his gaze is a fiery
cord. it cuts just as hard as his hands
against my cheeks, given with the
same casual violence.

behind his eyes,
a dull flame flickers, saying
"you make me what I am,
sinners and liars and restless sons".
he isn't a man to take responsibility
for anyone's humanity, weakness
the greatest abomination.

every nerve misfires along
their skin, his flock of lambs ready
to fling themselves up from the pews
and storm the pulpit, wage war
on the holy with fists of hymn books
and pockets full of mints.

tension builds, draws itself coiled
around the wool carpeted floor, rattles
the tall windows as people cough, rustle
pages together-anything to break
the weight sinking around them.

ready to cry, to shout out loud,
the congregation springs muscles
back as one great beast, a cat poised
to lunge when he lifts up his hands,

more glorious than Christ on Easter,
and proclaims

"hear my brothers, listen
my sisters to the word of the lord
for now, for now all you blind men,
you are saved by the grace immortal."

they swoon out to him. the organ
stutters to life and pounds out jubilation as,
like lovers spent, the congregation falls
into each other's arms.

after the service,
trapped in the sticky backseat
of a lumbering buick meandering along
farm roads, I listen to my mother
recount my physical transgressions.
every twitch, my legs swimming beneath
the pews, must be paid for in
midnight visits.

"why", he asks me,
turning to leave my room
as I gasp, fight for breath as pain
scatters along my ribs, "why don't you
just sit still during sunday service?"

seven years old
but even I knew
there was no safe answer.

how do you tell god
he doesn't scare you
anymore?

"Sooner or later even memory is taken, and we're not sure/
what remains. All we know is that the day is darker./
And something has had its fill."
-Sue Sinclair, Breaker, *In the Long Afternoons*

LINGERING

my father is sickness grown
quiet, turned inward as his blood passes
around the fatal poison. cancer watches
us from behind his eyes, our slow movements
as we gather him together, arms legs dreams
into one blanketed bed.

my sister is saying "let him sleep,"
when all he wants is to wake up
from his body's graceful betrayal,
the limbs gone soft and cheeks pulled
tight against the bone

even awake, he's not here
with us like before, his steady presence
was a wall and a floor, holding us in
and together from the moment
of our births

now a window, an open
door he keeps forgetting to close shut
as his memories come undone, clutter
up the room in layers of meaning, stagnant
with loss as he realizes time has
left him here alone

I think his spirit is traveling,
reaching back towards Michigan, the dirt roads
and backwoods of his distant childhood
where he learned to hunt, skin a rabbit,
gut a fish - all the knowledge of being an Indian
without ever saying the word.

even the dog is restless, circles from his side
to the door, as if to remind my father
not to leave without taking him along
for the ride.

we know he is dying,
can read the doctor's reluctance to offer
timelines as a certain promise
of his unraveling.

but still, we linger between hope
and loss like children waiting for the sounds
of a car in the driveway, only hearing the rush
of life moving past and counting down
the hours.

my father ignores our wavering,
grief and memory mingles with the sweetness
of narcotics, experimental drugs burning
through his vision as he sits and stares
out into the yard.

I want to ask him so many
things. the selfish questions of
love and need, explain his failures as a father
and the innumerable ways he fractured
my bones. the stories he never told,
about his mother and life on the land
among the traplines of her brothers. even
the regrets he carries, the pieces of him
never put to rest.

I want everything
of him - the scent of his aftershave,
the feel of his rough hands and the way
his eyes curve upward when he laughs -

not because he is lingering on
the doorstep to absence, not because
of the cancer coiling in his brain, not because
of love or the fear of things left
unsaid

like my dog, trying
to chase his scent in the breeze, cold snout up,
sniffing - I want to know
when he dies

what has gone
and what, if anything, remains
behind

LOVERS AND OTHER STRANGERS

ANSWERING MACHINE MESSAGE TO AN OLD LOVER

I'm so fucking tired
of pretending to be your silent witness.

just another part of the land
you step over, pass through like a spring thaw
melting winter's resolve.

I've become too complacent
in the heat of your gaze,
slow and stunned like a heavy beast
in the rut of your cock.

kept my mouth shut and tongue silent
as you strutted around, waving your belligerent hands
like beacons in the night, calling all the lost people
home to your temporary radiance.

if I said you were a shooting star,
I meant you lack stamina
but you've got the gift of misinterpretation,
don't you, baby?

call me easy but at least I'm not as cheap as you,
any good illusionist wins the four minute
drive of your affection, gets to send you home
in cabs drunk and talking big.

speaking of size, you're a gifted contortionist
where it counts, making mountains out of molehills
and coaxing your way into the warm dens
of strangers with an clever smile.

you know too much for me
to keep you around, but I can't get the stains
out of my quilts, like a deepening regret
which spreads with every washing.

've said too little
and now I've gone and said too much
from the covert protection of words
and finely minced bullshit

better luck next time,
find yourself a real Indian woman
who can fry your eggs
and skin your moose,
if you know what I mean.

I just called to let you know
your cheque is in the mail
and I've shot the dog.

please leave your key
behind the same old excuses
and think of me when you get jumped
in a dark alley.

DEATH THREAT

You decided to kill me,
in the shadows of an August evening,
the lake water itself a silent participant
in your murderous gaze.

hands on my right arm, pressing me
back off the shoreline, out into the cold expanse
of water and stars. I remember my own strength,
the power of blood and bone turned deaf,
mute to my calls to break your grip,
fight for what was mine.

Strange it would come to this,
you cloaked in your deadly rage, the selfish
lines of your desire more important than
my life.

A part of me wheels away from
the moment, refuses to engage it as truth,
but in nightly visitations, you return to remind me
how far we stepped over the edge of everything.

How dangerous you were,
how convinced of your own insight into meaning
that you could weave death freely without any threads snagging,
tearing on your hands.

My voice saved me. Remembering the first terrors,
I tried the familiar pleas learned from a childhood
of bruises. When you surrendered, released me
from your grip, I felt the old shame return
as if death was preferable to being
another victim.

Looking back, you must wonder

what it would have been like to have carried me over
into the water, held me under as my lungs swelled
and collapsed from pressure.

I regret never telling you what I thought,
standing there, trying to keep my footing on the edge
of everything.

Fear was absent, missing
from my limbs and in my mind.

There was only this: a great nothing
moving about in the lake, shadowing across the sky
and breathing on the wind.

LIARS

this morning,
caught up in the grips of another
cigarette craving, nicotine
breathing in your veins, you laughed
out loud, strong

and I missed you more
than before, the sureness in your voice
gone in the winter's long month, that dark
cloud of loss which swept over
everything

you keep giving advice,
pretending you're the one with all the cards
but it's been me, hasn't it, holding
the threads of your life still, teaching
you to breathe again

he takes his time leaving,
doesn't he, as you watch the shuffling
steps, catch his eyes peering out the window
into some impossible landscape you
could never follow him

a husband, a lover, a friend
dying each day, you burn the pieces
away in my smuggled smokes,
telling me life is always the same

just two bodies walking
down the horizon, dogging our steps
with the smell of old tobacco and sage
burned too quickly

give it up,
you tell me,
dreams are meant for better liars than us.

FAINTING

the first time I fainted
it was a revelation.

my skin forgetting itself,
turning me out instead of keeping
me in.

the sudden cold sweeping
against my hairs, burrowing in my
stomach and taking me
under.

even my throat,
hollow vessel of every human sound
I've ever made, constricted
away any chance of speaking
to the nurses moving past.

I saw the ceiling disintegrate
and open to the sky, my irises
consumed by light as if a window to the movement
of celestial bodies came unlatched.

I heard my mother's voice,
laughing as if from behind a closed door,
then nothing, all sensations numb.

when I woke, pulled my mind
from its tangled bundle of
sleep, the first thing I did
was count my breaths

determined to keep a grip
on what we, broken instruments
of nerves and tendons, can never hold
onto tightly enough to prevent from falling.

STRAIGHT LINE

You left with the first
of the snow. The heavy breath
of winter sending shivers
up my watery spine.

Like you once did, the slow passage
of your fine fingered hands charting the spaces
between my ribcage, the curve of my pelvis
a river splitting in the soft pressure
of your embrace.

Now, three springs have
come and gone. Still the cold
remembers my name, calls me
from the silvered tree leaves, those narrow
corridors of memory too tight to pass,
deep enough to drown
in.

Before I knew the color
of your eyes, the weight of your gaze
sunburnt on my skin - I thought love
was a straight line.

Like a child with
a bird in my hand,
I lifted your voice up to
the sky, cast you into the blue and waited
for the road to lead you back
to my bed.

You taught me otherwise. Love,
no simple animal driven by instinct,
more a shadow darting in the riverbed,
murky diver more felt than
seen.

You, a murmur in my bones,
always behind the curve
of vision. There and not there,
in my body and out of my
heart.

BREATH

when I think of you
everything slows down,
takes a breath and exhales
damp into the night

you used to be a roar
in my blood, skull laughing
between neurons and the quick
electricity of your glance, longing
an ember on my
tongue

couldn't wait to dissolve
in the horizon of bodies,
an unknown landscape of
wayward bones lying like
discarded timbers, your heartbeat
an underwater beacon I could dive
to, reach out with my hands, small
roots to ground our love.

the final shouts
rang in my ears like fists
thumping into wet soil,
all the effort amounting to nothing
as you left, a startled bird in flight,
wheeling away from me
in a mad arc

everything was consumed
by the urgency of our discovery, the profoundness
of young love, saying to our friends we'd found
something worth changing for, shallow earth
to dream on

so much life, lived too quick
and cast off in the careless belief
we could always summon
more from the waters, drink
our stubborn fill

what gets left behind
of our love? not the promises,
the battles won and lost,
our drunken sex as your girlfriend
canvassed the neighborhood, always knowing
but never meeting my eye

what remains of a love
like us, sharp on the curve of adulthood
but still hooked on the mythology
of our parents

only my breath has any answers,
nudges in the quiet way of bodies
and points me to the long center
of the lake, the coldest point where only
deep breaths carry any chance
of touching the bottom

"A nihilist is a man who judges of the world as it is that it ought not to be, and of the world as it ought to be that it does not exist."

-Friedrich Nietzsche, *KSA* 12:9 [60]

PHILOSOPHY

she is a lesson
in motion.

her entire life comprises
of moving forward, reaching back along
the narrow ridge of ancestors, her culture
a road to follow up, the traditions
we've inherited more a blade
to grasp than a covent to keep.

me, the curve in a river
where everything gets stuck, the ringed pool
of dead branches, shallow yellow water
waiting for a heavy rain

drunk and talking loud,
we once discussed the meaning of life.

she was certain of its dimensions,
the character of all things reduced to a solid
center you could build a life around.

I want the same clarity, the promise
of a life walked with deliberate steps.
an answer to end the questions,
the great restlessness of minds
ended by seeing the invisible
god.

when I told her this, about
my inability to become anything more
or less, she laughed and told me
I was a nihilist.

maybe I am,
but she'll never know the sweet taste of bracken,
of the tiny life growing in the cervices beside
the rushing water, where only stagnation can shelter
possibility.

sometimes
movement only carries you past
the loss. there are wounds the
body cannot run fast nor far enough
to heal. any child knows

it's the nothing that
holds the mystery
of transformation.

RECOLLECTION

For Dusky

"that sometimes we don't ask enough, full of desire
and thinking ourselves visible by its brilliance alone,
that loss like birth pushes us again and again
toward some unknown and unsought country"

-Maureen Harris, Drowning Lessons, "*A Form of Falling*"

I want you to know I remember
everything.

If my mind was a river, you could
step over me into a forest
filled by low cedars and every space
between the branches would be
your absence.

The last few days,
tired in the heavy evening, my mind has moved
across the dusk to call
your memory, translucent
and still solid, a weight around my skin
I can barely bear.

recall the river, more a lake
curving around the city like a serpent
caught in midday heat. the water, gathering
your body, moving between sunlight
and undercurrent.

the sound of your voice echoing
out across open water, a billow of noise
flinging into the corners of my body,
resonance in bone dryly
murmuring your name again
and again.

should I be grateful for loving you,
a submerged body rendered visible
by your memory alone?

I want you to know
as clearly as a knife through a tendon, I remember
everything but most of all,
you.

GOOD THE DARK

BECOMING

what becomes us
in the fall from dusk to dawn,
those heavy hours of searching in the shallows
of memory for smooth pieces of regret
to hold then throw away into
the current.

who is the disquiet voice
speaking out of turn and refusing
to let sleep take away the rustling of words
we have not and will never say to each other,
the tongue of absence marking perfectly
in the language of loss what remains
unsaid in everything.

where have they risen from,
the ghostly skeletons pantomiming a slow dance across the floor
as if to say, come and embrace us as the music stutters out half-
hearted apologies
and whispers the names we have written
on the corridors of our bodies.

why do we call ourselves human,
meaning creatures who are free from blind instinct
and consider ourselves proud to shit sitting down,
when all we have managed to achieve is to imprison desire
in the photocopy brilliance of morning?

it is the night which becomes us,
holds our limbs still while the mind is consumed by vision
and desire, resurrects the buried bodies of the past,

the murmuring bones that do not decay
under time's numbing touch, becoming more polished
and translucent, captivating to the eye
and pleasing to the hands so that we are never
rid of them.

WHAT LIVES IN ME

what lives in me,
those long hours alone in the dark
as I hunt the deep water
for words?

the tongues I speak
are not mine, distant echoes
of some great disaster I cannot name
without falling silent.

I could say I possess my body,
but how many times have I been taken
by the desires of others, those beasts of burden
come home to strain against my skin?

I am my ancestors' child,
they traded away land and life
for a few small beads, tricked by survival's plaintive logic
into surrendering the things which made them human.

instead of people,
I have stories. my longing has turned
against the natural order, I seek nothing
but answers to questions which no one
has asked.

what is left to live in me,
after so many years afraid and small
in the shadow of my father's anger,
my mother's indifference?

I look around me
and find only books. I raise my voice
and no sound emerges but the rustling of pages,
stacks of poetry unwritten and too many things left unsaid.

the weight of language crushes me,
I drown in the consonants of memory
and there is no one left to save me
from myself.

BONES

let the bones loose,
out of their wooden keepers
and tumbled across the floor of the living.

see where they land,
the hollow cysts of memory
which grew in your ancestors' flesh
like milky seeds in an earthy bog.

read the calcium depressions,
the yellowed marks of age are a doorway
you cannot open without first shutting the windows
and turning the lights off.

let everything shake itself out,
dazed and confused as the brittle pieces
make their own music in the night.

you have carried them too long
in the leather hide of your chest
to let them lie silent, unmoving in your selfish desire
for peace.

spread them out on the living room table,
across bedspreads and on window ledges,
their bones will protect you from forgetting yourself
and you owe them this small thing.

after all, the bones knew you first
in the wet cradle of your mother's body,
and it is their cracked tongues which will sing
as you stumble past the water's edge into nothing
when life abandons you.

INHERITANCE

what remains in us
is only what has been given
by the heavy step of our ancestors
walking along the darkened trap lines,
searching for the offerings of the day.

we speak no new tongues
and tell no different stories.
everything repeats
in our mouths, turns over like a stone
between the teeth which cannot be
swallowed.

we burn our fires in the ashes
of the past, calling each moment
by a new name, never realizing the constants
which bind our memories belonged to the dead
before we ever spoke them.

we think the dead have come
from a great darkness which sits apart
from the world of the living.

how stubborn our ignorance,
determined to keep our ancestors from us
and denying the voices of the body.

the inheritance is double in us,
we are the heirs of death
and the promised ones
who will die.

FORGIVENESS

forgive your ancestors
their small sins.

they broke promises across your skin,
made you afraid in the night by talking drunk
and chain smoking in the kitchen without apology.

once or twice an uncle or cousin let their hands
wander past the lines of what could be considered appropriate
and your parents laughed it off and pushed you out into the yard
to play.

maybe your grandfather was monster with his leather belt,
beating the air restless in your father's home
as he broke bones and delusions with heavy fists.

your grandmother might have been a coward,
who let everything slide by her as she retreated,
said nothing while he raged through her children's bodies
like a drought, a sweltering wind of fire and blight

but your ancestors are no more, no less
than the sum of you, made up of the same soil
and waters as your descendant flesh

if you can forgive them the greater and lesser abominations,
you can begin to understand
the burden of apology

how it requires precision, detailed inventories
like a storeroom clerk with a notepad, clicking off items
and demanding receipts

the easy answer is not to forgive your ancestors
but feast their bones with the only offering
which can still move them

it is enough to remember
and speak of them in every dark place
you can find.

GO HOME NOW

time for the dead to slumber
in the somnolent night of forgetting,
quiet as school children in class
as they wait for the bell to ring,
releasing them from this painful audience
of lectures and lessons delivered by rote.

see them walking side by side through corridors
of smoke and lake water, trailing cloaks of algae
like world weary whales turning into the cold current
of the atlantic, away from fishing boats and plastic nets
to find another life secret from the eyes of japanese tourists
in the mysterious deep of places human minds have not conquered.

noiseless in the early morning light, dawn fire imbuing
the pale outlines so that the dead appear as strangers
behind the sheer curtains of everything that wants to be
a part of this vainglorious new world, how they shift away
from the point of observation, steal the offerings
like scavengers of life, hungry orphans amid the ruins
of our great cities, cast away families and lovers disappearing.

we have a little less wonder but perhaps more freedom
than we did when they stood beside us because who wants
to feel the weight of centuries on their shoulders as they shop
for another sofa, heavy lidded justification for wanting to sleep
without their constant intrusions, the demands they make of our memory
as if nothing will satisfy their love of sorrow, how much they want to drink
our grief like drunken dock workers turning up on payday with a fist full of twenties.

they're packing up the picnic of corpses, stowing away the sandwiches
and dashing for the departing train, giving up the ghost in old buildings and churches
taking their stories with them like angry poets at a small scale reading downtown

letting go of everything we ever placed in their amphoral hands, throwing out the letters and shoving off from the shore line in their 400 horsepower boats, cutting through the breakers like a knife through the soft inner flesh, leaving us alone with ourselves again.

how long will they be gone, no one knows, but goddamn it, isn't that just like the dead to go and leave you hanging, dreaming of some small sign of their continued vibrancy, holding on and hoping for something, anything, to make life feel less lonely, as if you could lift up the earth and find everything you ever lost, waiting.

GOOD THE DARK

how beautiful the night,
good the dark, gentle the moon.

how rich the promise of stars,
shining though pale sheets of memory
and distance.

like us, their brilliance grows
the farther they are from home
and death only makes them
appear brighter in the irises
of the sky.

we have much to learn
from the nightly voices
about how the heart is
a nocturnal bloomer

how the dead wait
for us beneath the clouds
and step through our dreams
like ghostly fireflies dancing past
the reach of our clumsy eyes

how much life is hidden
in the darkness we fear,
the familiar faces we miss
when we turn from the window
to stare blindly into the fire.

how we sleep, the dead and living,
in the arms of the night sky,
swaying in the winds
and singing soft

how beautiful the night,
good the dark, gentle the moon.

ACKNOWLEDGEMENTS

This collection would not have been possible without the work of several important people: Cherie Dimaline, Lee Maracle, Daniel Heath Justice, Joanne Argue, and Neal McLeod. Thank you for your support, editorial guidance, and for believing in the work before anyone else.

To Kegedonce Press, Kateri and Renee, for your outstanding support and vision about this collection.

To those who have supported my development as a writer: Douglas Macgregor, Peter Luscombe, Victoria Freeman, and Aaron Jankowski.

To those who taught me about our culture and world-view: Alex M, Douglas W, Shirley W, Brian N., Mark and Wendy P, Vern D, Joseph N., and so many others who have worked to maintain our languages and ceremonies despite the continued challenges.

To my family in this world and the next, thank you for the memories of our lives, as well as understanding that some stories have to be told, no matter how painful it may be to speak them.

To Cherie, for hours of swapping stories, providing constant encouragement, doing hundreds of tiny edits, chain smoking menthols, and for being an uppity 'breed' with me at every possible occasion.

To Alex, for telling me that all stories come from longing and that there is no shame in longing for your ancestors.

To Lee, for telling me that the dead are more powerful than living.

And most importantly, to the dead. You have never forgotten your responsibilities to the living, even when we have forgotten our responsibilities to you.

Kinanaakomin. We are grateful.

ABOUT THE AUTHOR:

Giles (Mitikomis) Benaway (Anishinaabe/Tsagli/Métis) is
of Odawa/Potawatomi, Cherokee, British, and Anglo Métis
descent. His paternal ancestors are from Walpole Island and
Northern Michigan, as his Métis forefathers migrated to
the region. His maternal ancestors are original Mayflower
immigrants who settled in West Virginia and worked as coal
miners in Raleigh County for more than three centuries.
Currently working on his second poetry collection and a young
adult novel about a teenaged gay Aboriginal werewolf with
Asperger's Syndrome, he lives in Toronto, Ontario.